■SCHOLAS

VOCABULARY-BOOSTING JOKES & RIDDLES

Fast & Fun Rib-Ticklers That Teach Kids More Than 100 Great New Words!

by Justin McCory Martin

New York • Toronto • London • Auckland • Sydney
Mexico City • New Delhi • Hong Kong • Buenos Aires

Teaching *Resources*

To Eric Charlesworth, who is going pro—
as in, becoming a professional teacher

Cover design by Jim Sarfati and Jaime Lucero
Cover illustrations by Jeff Moores
Interior design by Solutions by Design, Inc.
Interior illustrations by Mike Moran

ISBN: 0-439-54256-1

2 3 4 5 6 7 8 9 10   40   11 10 09 08 07 06 05 04

Contents

Introduction

Looking for a way to expand students' vocabularies and have a chuckle in the process? This collection of more than 100 jokes and riddles features vocabulary words in a format that helps kids really learn and remember new words and their meanings. Here are some examples:

- ▣ Why did the kid eat all his green vegetables? To **appease** his dad.

- ▣ What do you call a humorous athlete? **Jocular**.

- ▣ What does celery do when it's in a hurry? It **accelerates**.

Making vocabulary words the punch lines to jokes is a great memory-boosting strategy. Such mnemonic devices help students learn and retrieve information by using humorous and often silly associations. For example, adults who grew up in the 1970s still find themselves humming songs from *Schoolhouse Rock* in order to remember conjunctions, or picturing a large letter *R* sawing a small stone in order to remember that Little Rock is the capital of Arkansas. Kids will enjoy hearing the jokes and they'll enjoy sharing them with friends and family—another incentive to remember the words. It all adds up to making language acquisition fun and memorable.

Each joke is presented on a reproducible card that contains everything you need to introduce and reinforce the vocabulary word. Let's let another vegetable illustrate how the cards work: What do you call an onion that likes to get into mischief? Answer: A **rapscallion**.

Each word is accompanied by an effective writing prompt that encourages kids to think and write about the words they're learning. This not only provides additional reinforcement of the words' meanings, but it also gives kids a chance to put pen to paper and hone their writing skills. The various prompts challenge students to use these new words in short stories, poems, rap songs, advertising jingles, e-mails, diary entries, and much more.

Educators have long realized the importance of a rich vocabulary in the development of strong reading and writing skills, but making vocabulary acquisition engaging can sometimes be a challenge. Rote memorization of words and definitions often does not lead to long-term learning. By making the process fun and even a little bit silly, you can give kids a way to make connections and really remember new words. Best of all, vocabulary jokes and riddles help students see how enjoyable language and word play can be.

How to Use This Book

The vocabulary jokes and riddles in this book are organized by general topics—food, animals, jobs and hobbies, style and shopping, and more—but you can present them in any order. (For quick reference, words are also listed alphabetically on page 10 with corresponding joke page numbers.)

You might select jokes at random, or choose groups of jokes to present as a set. Either way, presenting one or two jokes a day is a good way to give students a chance to absorb each new word. There are many ways to choose jokes and group them together. Here are some suggestions:

- Select jokes that relate to a particular area of study or a current event. (For example, mysteries: **incognito**, **sleuth**, **grime**; sports: **jocular**, **waver**, **jersey**, **slugfest**, **underdog**, **fowl**)

- Choose a set of jokes with vocabulary words that are related to one another in some way (for example, moods: **glum**, **tranquil**, **moody**, and **melancholy**).

- Present jokes that feature vocabulary words that are all the same part of speech (for example, verbs: **appease**, **grapple**, **detest**, and **embellish**).

- Choose jokes with writing prompts of the same genre (for example, storytelling prompts: **melancholy**, **parable**, **pickle**, **wile**; dialogue prompts: **truculent**, **jocular**, **mutter**, **rapscallion**; and letter-writing prompts: **inhospitable**, **ultimatum**, **appease**, **notable**).

Presenting Jokes

Give students a quick and easy dose of word humor by making an overhead transparency of the joke and displaying it in the morning, after lunch, or any other time of the day. Have them read the joke and respond to the writing prompt. You might have students keep ongoing vocabulary journals in which they can record new words, definitions, and responses to writing prompts (see Extension Activities, page 6).

Another approach is to photocopy and cut apart the cards. Give students a copy of the individual cards so that they can compile a collection of jokes. Once they have collected ten or more jokes, have them staple the pages together to form a mini-book. You might present these words on a short quiz.

However you choose to present the jokes, allow time to discuss the vocabulary words. Provide examples of how to use the words in context and encourage students to think of their own examples. Expand the topic by discussing related words, such as synonyms or antonyms. On many of the cards, you'll find additional words listed under Vocab Boost. Review these words with students to help them understand how the vocabulary words might be used as different parts of speech, or to learn meanings of other words included in the joke or writing prompt.

EXTENSION ACTIVITIES

The following activities are intended to provide reinforcement of vocabulary words that have already been introduced to students. This repeated exposure to the words helps students retain the meanings.

Vocabulary Journals

Have students create journals in which they can keep track of the new words they're learning from the jokes, as well as from other sources. In their journals, students can also record their responses to writing prompts, draw illustrations that will help them remember a word's meaning, and write their own vocabulary jokes. You might give students copies of the joke card templates (page 9), on which they can record and illustrate their jokes. Add these to a classroom display.

Research Projects

If you choose to present a set of jokes on the same theme, have students research and present short reports on a related topic. For example, students could research nutrition for food jokes, ocean life for sea creatures, careers for jobs and hobbies, and so on. Encourage students to incorporate as many new vocabulary words into their reports as they can. This is a fun way to reinforce words, and it can lead to some humorous reporting.

Vocation Exploration

After presenting all or some of the jokes on careers and hobbies, hold a "classroom career week." Have students choose a job as the subject of a short research report. As part of their report, challenge students to come up with a list of ten words that relate to the profession they chose. (Encourage them to be creative in their word associations.) In addition, show students the Help Wanted section of a newspaper and read aloud a few job advertisements. Challenge students to write an ad for their job that includes a few vocabulary words. Have a few students present their reports and ads each day.

Bulletin Boards

When presenting jokes by topic, create a thematic bulletin board on which to display the jokes. For example, to present the fruits and veggies jokes, make a display that looks like a grocery store produce section. From craft paper, cut out large, colorful fruits and vegetables, or clip photos from a magazine or supermarket circular. Display the jokes in the appropriate area of your "produce section." Encourage students to think of their own fruit and vegetable jokes and add them to the display. For dog jokes, create a bulletin board that looks like a fancy dog-grooming store. Display the jokes alongside photos or drawings of various dogs. You might emphasize the words and definitions by writing them on paper dog bowls or dog tags. Other bulletin board ideas include a zoo for animal jokes, a shopping mall for style and shopping, an underwater scene for sea creatures, and a dinner table for food jokes.

Wordy Newspaper

Have students work in small groups to create a short newspaper. Discuss the different sections of a newspaper, such as top stories, sports, letters to the editor, advertisements, advice columns, comics, and so on. Give each group a list of vocabulary words to include in their newspapers (encourage them to be creative). Once students have finished, create a newsstand that students can visit to peruse the vocabulary-boosting periodicals.

Picture Match

Choose vocabulary words you have covered in class and write them on index cards (one word per card). Then cut out photographs, ads, cartoons, or other printed material from magazines or newspapers that relate to the words in some way (either directly or, for more of a challenge, indirectly). Create four or five sets of different pictures and words and store them in large envelopes. Divide the class into small groups and give each group an envelope. Challenge the groups to match the words and pictures and explain how they are related. For example, you might provide the following words and printed material:

Adorable—Photo of babies

Chic—Ad from fashion magazine

Frugal—Coupon

Notable—Photo of a famous artist

Rambunctious—Photo of playful puppies

Comic Relief

Give students an opportunity to present vocabulary jokes as stand-up comedians. Playing with words and using them orally will help students remember new words and feel comfortable using them in conversation. In addition to presenting jokes, students can also create their own skits that feature vocabulary words. Some ideas include a talk show on which a host interviews guests, a news report in which newscasters present school or community news, a game show, and so on. Consider organizing an informal performance for another class or grade level. Not only will this enhance students' vocabulary skills, it will also provide them with practice in public speaking.

Alliterative Animals

Have students collaborate to create a zany zoo of alliterative animals. Assign a few letters of the alphabet to small groups, pairs, or individual students. Challenge each group to write a short description or story about an animal whose name begins with an assigned letter (alligator, bear, camel, and so on). Explain that students should include as many words that begin with the same letter as they can, and to use vocabulary words or other interesting words. (Keep dictionaries and thesauruses on hand for this assignment.) When they are finished, have students read aloud their stories while classmates record the featured words they hear.

Poetry Slam

Here's a way to connect vocabulary to your poetry studies. Provide students with a list of vocabulary words and ask them to choose a few to feature in a poem. The poem could include the word, or it could be about the word. Have students experiment with creating different types of poetry, asking them to include some of their new words in the poem. (A good starting point for this activity would be the writing prompt which accompanies the joke for **tranquil**. This prompt introduces haiku and also explains the typical tone and mood of poems in this genre.) After writing some haikus, you might have students experiment with concrete poems, in which the words on the page take a shape that relates to the subject of the poem. Other poetic forms might include limericks, sonnets, acrostics, or cinquains.

Picture Practice

Encourage students to take a closer look at the illustrations included with each joke. Discuss how the illustration connects to the vocabulary word. Challenge students to draw their own cartoon depicting the same joke. For example, after reading the **rapscallion** joke, ask students: "What's another way a scallion could cause mischief in the produce section?" Or you might extend the assignment to have students illustrate a different scenario with the same vocabulary word. For example, the illustration for **appease** shows a young boy eating all his vegetables to please his dad. Ask: "How else might a kid appease a parent?"

Story Pass

In this pass-along collaborative story, students have a chance to use some of the new words they have learned. Write a list of vocabulary words on a sheet of paper. Explain that each student will add a few sentences to the story and must include at least one vocabulary word from the list. Ask students to check off words that they have used. Explain that the goal is to use all the words. If a student is stuck, he or she can use one of the words that has already been checked off. Have the first student look at the list and write a few sentences to start the story. The student then passes the story to the next student, who adds a few more sentences. The process continues until every student has contributed and every word on the list is used. Remind students that the story should have a beginning, middle, and ending.

Mystery Word Game

Write vocabulary words on index cards (one word per card). Have each student randomly select a card. Explain that students should use a thesaurus to write a series of five cryptic clues about their word. They will read one clue at a time, allowing classmates to guess the word after hearing each clue. Explain that the clues should not be too obvious and should get their classmates thinking. Another variation of this is to have students draw a picture to represent their word or act it out while classmates guess. These games can be played as a class or in two teams.

Vocabulary-Enhancing Inventions

Let students work in small groups on this creative writing assignment. Ask each group to make up an invention that can be used to improve writing. Encourage students to be detailed in their explanations and use specific examples to show how their products work. Have groups name their machines and draw pictures of them. You might have groups write jingles or advertisements for their new products, build prototypes, or sketch advertising campaigns. Some suggestions to get ideas flowing might include the following:

> **Synonym Sorcerer**—a machine that takes in simple words and releases better, bigger words with the same meaning
>
> **Antonymator**—a machine that replaces a word with its opposite
>
> **Banality Buster**—A handy homework tool that identifies boring words and phrases

JOKE: _____

ANSWER: _____

_____ (_____): _____
word   part of speech   definition

Writing Prompt _____
_____

In the box, illustrate your joke.

_____
_____

VOCAB BOOST _____ (_____):
word   part of speech

_____
definition

JOKE: _____

ANSWER: _____

_____ (_____): _____
word   part of speech   definition

Writing Prompt _____
_____

In the box, illustrate your joke.

_____
_____

VOCAB BOOST _____ (_____):
word   part of speech

_____
definition

Word List

Vocabulary words appear in jokes on the pages listed below.

What do you call a humorous athlete?

ANSWER: **Jocular**

jocular (adjective): full of jokes and good humor

 Writing Prompt Imagine two characters named Jocular Jess and Somber Sal. They are friends, but they are complete opposites. Jocular Jess is always laughing and playing pranks. Somber Sal is always very serious. Write some dialogue for the two friends. This will help you get started.

Jocular Jess: Knock, knock.

Somber Sal: I had better answer the door.

Jocular Jess: No, no, Somber Sal. I'm trying to tell a knock-knock joke!

 VOCAB BOOST **jock (noun):** an athlete or someone who enjoys sports
somber (adjective): serious and even rather gloomy

What do you call a rude nurse?

ANSWER: **Inhospitable**

inhospitable (adjective): unfriendly and impolite to guests

 Writing Prompt Pretend you write an advice column in the newspaper. You receive the following letter: "I really like my friend Pat. But whenever I visit, Pat's brothers and sisters are always very inhospitable. What should I do? —Frustrated in Fresno." Write back and give this person some good advice. This will help you get started: "Dear Frustrated in Fresno, I think you should…"

 VOCAB BOOST **hospitable (adjective):** friendly, generous, and welcoming to guests

What do you call a bunch of actors stuck on an island?

ANSWER: Castaways

castaway (noun): a person who is stranded on a desert island

 Writing Prompt Imagine that you are a castaway, shipwrecked on an island. You have only five possessions: a mirror, a coconut shell, some balloons, a pack of gum, and a roll of twine. How will you survive? Can you somehow use your possessions to get rescued?

VOCAB BOOST **cast (noun):** the group of actors in a play, movie, or television show

What word sounds like *vacation* but really means a kind of job?

ANSWER: Vocation

vocation (noun): a job, especially one for which a person is well suited

 Writing Prompt Have you ever had anyone ask you, "What do you want to be when you grow up?" That question generally means "What vocation will you choose?" Do you want to be a nurse, a violinist, a rodeo clown, a firefighter, a lawyer, a writer? There are certainly tons of vocations to choose from. Write about one that you would like to pursue. Explain what appeals to you about the job and why it would be a good fit for you.

Why was Sam the Spy dressed as Dr. Morito?
He was traveling incog_____.

ANSWER: Incognito

incognito (adjective and adverb):
hiding one's true identity, often using a disguise

 Write a short spy story. As a twist, have one of the characters go incognito. A spy could dress as a lion tamer in order to sneak into a circus. Or an evil villain, being chased by the spy, could dress as a police officer and pretend to be good. You decide: When characters go incognito, all kinds of fun twists are possible.

What did the surfer do when she saw the giant wave?

ANSWER: She wavered.

waver (verb): to be uncertain, especially about a decision; to tremble

 Have you ever wavered over a decision? Maybe you couldn't decide between vanilla ice cream and toffee pistachio swirl. If you're wavering, here's a good way to make up your mind. Make lists of "pluses" and "minuses." For example, some pluses of vanilla might be that it's a familiar flavor. Minuses might be that it's boring and there's already a box of vanilla ice cream at home in your freezer. Think of a decision that causes you to waver. Then create plus and minus lists. Try to include at least five pluses and minuses.

What do you call an unlucky beauty queen?

ANSWER: Misfortune

misfortune (noun): bad luck; an unfortunate event

Writing Prompt Create a speech for Misfortune, winner of this year's Boo-Hoo Pageant. This will help you get started: "Thank you, everyone. I feel so very unlucky to be named Misfortune. As I was walking up to accept this award, something awful happened...."

VOCAB BOOST **fortunate (adjective):** lucky
unfortunate (adjective): unlucky

What did the chef do when he ran out of pots?

ANSWER: He panicked.

panic (verb): to experience extreme fright and anxiety

 Writing Prompt Turn on a radio or play a CD in your classroom. Your teacher might also read a passage from a book. On a blank sheet of paper, write every word you hear as quickly as you can. This is a tough exercise. You have to listen carefully, write quickly, and above all, don't panic! See how accurately you can record what you hear. Good luck.

 VOCAB BOOST **panic (noun):** a sudden feeling of extreme anxiety or fear

...te eye named Ruth?

ANSWER: **Ruth the Sleuth**

sleuth (noun): a detective

 Apparently, Jimmy has lost his homework assignment. He spent the entire previous evening writing a paper on the Grand Canyon. It was in his backpack when he set off for school. It's the "Case of the Missing Homework." What happened? Write a detective story in which Ruth the Sleuth solves the case.

VOCAB BOOST **sleuth (verb):** to look for information

Why did the detective rope off the closet filled with dirty laundry?

ANSWER: **He was a grime stopper.**

grime (noun): dirt or filth

 Imagine that there is a new cleaning fluid called Grimebuster. Create a TV advertisement to help sell this product. This will help you get started: "The grime has got to go! For just $5.99, Grimebuster cleans up all kinds of messes...."

VOCAB BOOST **grimy (adjective):** dirty

What does celery do when it's in a hurry?

ANSWER: **It accelerates!**

accelerate (verb): to speed up

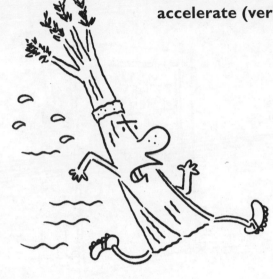

Writing Prompt Create an Accelerated Tale. Allow yourself exactly five minutes. Then write as interesting a story as possible. Try to include a beginning, middle, and ending. You'll need to make your story fast paced in order to finish it in such a short time. Ready, set, go!

What do you call a final warning given to a naughty tomato?

ANSWER: **An ultimatum**

ultimatum (noun): a final request, condition, or demand

Writing Prompt Stu will not stop taking your bicycle. He never asks permission. Sometimes he's gone for hours, using your bike when you want to ride it. The other day it rained and he kept the bike at his house overnight. When you woke up in the morning and couldn't find your bike, you worried that someone had stolen it. But it was just Stu "borrowing" your bicycle again.

You've talked to Stu about his behavior in the past. Now it's time for an ultimatum. If he takes the bike again, what will you do? Write Stu a letter in which you explain your frustration and spell out a firm but reasonable ultimatum.

What do you call a really heavy cucumber?

ANSWER: Cumbersome

cumbersome (adjective): large or heavy; difficult to carry

 Imagine a world in which light objects have suddenly become cumbersome. What if you were suddenly surrounded by heavy feathers, boulderlike pebbles, and ten-pound pencils? Write a story about this environment in which everything is cumbersome.

What kind of story did the pear tell the apple?

ANSWER: A parable

parable (noun): a story that teaches a moral or lesson

 King Midas was granted a magical power. Everything he touched turned to gold. At first he was happy, but when he tried to eat, his problems began. All his food kept turning to gold. So he begged for the power to be taken away. King Midas's story is a parable. It teaches the lesson that there can be too much of a good thing. Write your own parable. At the end, reveal the lesson it teaches.

What kind of question does a berry ask?

ANSWER: **A query**

query (noun): a question

 Writing Prompt What if you could ask anything of anyone—a real person or an imaginary character, someone alive today or someone from history. Think of a query and write it in the form of an e-mail. For example, a query for Thomas Jefferson might begin, "Dear Mr. Jefferson: I would like to know…" Then imagine how this person might have answered. Write an e-mail response to your own query.

VOCAB BOOST **query (verb):** to ask a question

How would you describe an unhappy plum?

ANSWER: **Glum**

glum (adjective): sad and gloomy

 Writing Prompt Imagine a character named Glum Griselda who is constantly in a dismal state of mind. Dream up an unhappy adventure for Griselda. When you write about her, make sure that she's suitably whiny and full of complaints.

 VOCAB BOOST **gloomy (adjective):** dark and dreary; depressed

Vocabulary-Boosting Jokes & Riddles Scholastic Teaching Resources

How do monkeys feel about bananas?

ANSWER: **They find them appealing.**

appealing (adjective): attractive; desirable; pleasing

Writing Prompt Imagine you own a restaurant. Create a menu which includes appetizing descriptions of the food. Say chicken noodle soup is one of your dishes. You could describe it on the menu as "a delicious soup with hearty chunks of fresh chicken and silky smooth noodles." Now that sounds appealing!

VOCAB BOOST **peel (noun):** the skin of a fruit or vegetable

Why did the kid eat all his green vegetables?

ANSWER: **To appease his dad.**

appease (verb): to soothe or calm

 Writing Prompt Your best friend is furious because you gave away a secret. Write a letter in which you apologize and explain why you made this mistake. Maybe you thought the secret wasn't that big a deal. Or maybe you can convince the person you told not to tell anyone else. When you write this letter, though, remember that the most important thing is that you appease your best friend.

What do you call it when an avocado pretends to act brave?

ANSWER: **Bravado**

bravado (noun): false and overconfident bravery

 Imagine acts of bravado by various fruits and vegetables. For example, a banana that's full of bravado might say: "Who are you calling unappealing? I'm going to call a bunch of my banana friends. We'll lie down on the floor and make you slip!" Write five short speeches by fruits and vegetables that are full of bravado.

What kind of problem does a cucumber have?

ANSWER: **A pickle**

pickle (noun): a tricky situation (informal);
a food that has been preserved in vinegar or salt water

 When someone is in a difficult situation with no easy solution in sight, we might say he or she is "in a pickle." Where do you think this saying came from? Write a short story describing the origins of this expression. Be creative!

 pickle (verb):
to preserve cucumbers or other foods in vinegar or salt water

Why didn't the farmer harvest his crop?

ANSWER: **He scorned it.**

scorn (verb): to show extreme distaste toward someone or something; to reject or refuse

Writing Prompt Imagine that you're watching TV and you see an advertisement for a new product called Super Cod Liver Oil–Flavored Edible Sunglasses. Write down some of your thoughts about this ridiculous invention. After all, something this silly deserves to be scorned.

VOCAB BOOST **scorn (noun):** a feeling of disrespect and distaste; open hatred

What is an apple doing when it's trying to solve a problem?

ANSWER: **Grappling**

grapple (verb): to struggle, especially with a problem; to wrestle

Writing Prompt What is a problem you have dealt with in the past? How did you solve it? What were some of the solutions you considered? Why did you choose the one you did? Write some "Helpful Hints" so that other people grappling with the same problem can learn from your experience.

What do you call an eager seal?

ANSWER: A seal filled with _____!

zeal (noun): enthusiasm

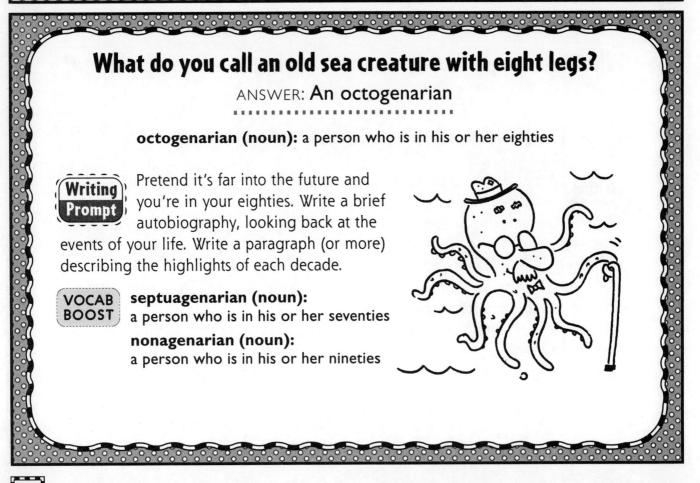

Writing Prompt

Zeal and *zest* are a pair of *z* words that have roughly the same meaning: great enthusiasm. What is something about which you feel zest and zeal? Write a song in which you capture your excitement.

VOCAB BOOST **zealous (adjective):** filled with enthusiasm

What do you call an old sea creature with eight legs?

ANSWER: An octogenarian

octogenarian (noun): a person who is in his or her eighties

Writing Prompt

Pretend it's far into the future and you're in your eighties. Write a brief autobiography, looking back at the events of your life. Write a paragraph (or more) describing the highlights of each decade.

VOCAB BOOST

septuagenarian (noun): a person who is in his or her seventies

nonagenarian (noun): a person who is in his or her nineties

What do you call algae that yearns for the past?

ANSWER: **Nostalgic**

nostalgic (adjective): longing for the past; homesick

 Writing Prompt
Do you ever feel nostalgic? If you don't now, bet you will in the year 2050. Perhaps you'll think fondly about your old grade school, your old friends, music you listened to, or TV shows you used to watch. Imagine you're creating a time capsule. Write about the objects you would place in it and why. A time capsule would sure come in handy in 2050 when you're feeling nostalgic, don't you think?

VOCAB BOOST **yearn (verb):** to wish for or want something

What kind of noise do you hear in a seafood shop?

ANSWER: **Clamor**

clamor (noun): loud sounds; shouting

 Writing Prompt
There are a variety of words to describe loud sounds: *shriek*, *howl*, *bang*, and *boom* are just a few. Write a Clamorous Tale in which all kinds of noisy things happen.

VOCAB BOOST **clamor (verb):** to make noise; to demand loudly

clamorous (adjective): noisy, loud

What kind of song does a person with a cold sing?

ANSWER: **A malady**

malady (noun): sickness or other symptom of poor health

Writing Prompt Write your own Malady Melody about having a cold. Create a song in which you describe how you feel and what you do to get better. Set the lyrics to a familiar tune.

VOCAB BOOST **melody (noun):** the tune of a song

lyrics (noun): the words of a song

What instrument thinks it outranks the rest?

ANSWER: **The trumpet**

trump (verb): to top, get the best of, or outrank

Writing Prompt Create a Trump List. Here's an example: "Chocolate trumps vanilla. Vanilla trumps butterscotch. Butterscotch trumps hazelnut." See how long you can go with a single Trump List. Or else create several of them in different categories such as foods, TV shows, and sports.

Why did the band stop making music?

ANSWER: **It was defunct.**

defunct (adjective): no longer in existence

Writing Prompt The word *defunct* is used to describe something that no longer exists. The word *defrost* means to remove frost. Then there's *deflate*, which means to let out the air. It's the opposite of *inflate*. Oftentimes, the prefix *de-* is used in words in which something is removed or reversed. Write a "*De-* Story," a story using lots of words that start with *de-*.

VOCAB BOOST **funk (noun):** a type of rhythmic music that's part blues, part soul, and part jazz

---

What did Violet say when she found her lost viola?

ANSWER: **Voilà!**

voilà (interjection): used to draw attention to an accomplishment or something that has suddenly appeared

Writing Prompt *Voilà* is a fun word. It's French, but it's such a great word that English speakers borrowed it. It roughly means "Hey, will you look at this!" Here's an example of how the word is used: "I cut out a coupon from a magazine, mailed it in, and—*voilà!*—here are my new 3-D goggles." Now, use *voilà* in a short story.

What do you call it when piano keys are in agreement?

ANSWER: **Accord**

accord (noun): agreement, usually between people in conflict

 Okay, here's the situation: A foul-tempered pirate, a dramatic opera singer, and a nine-year-old computer whiz are trapped at the top of a roller coaster. If they start fighting, they'll have trouble getting to safety. They need to be in accord. Write the story of how they work together to get out of this pickle.

 chord (noun): a combination of musical sounds or notes, such as three piano keys being struck at once

Why did the violinist get so many fan letters?

ANSWER: **She was notable.**

notable (adjective): worthy of great interest

 Who do you think is especially remarkable? It could be someone you know, someone who is famous, or someone from the past. Write a letter to that person, explaining what you admire about him or her. What about this person is notable?

VOCAB BOOST **notable (noun):** an important person; one who is well known

Vocabulary-Boosting Jokes & Riddles Scholastic Teaching Resources

How would you describe a stylish barnyard bird?

ANSWER: **Chic** (pronounced SHEEK)

chic (adjective): stylish and fashionable

 Pretend that you are the announcer for a fashion show for farm animals. Describe each animal's stylish outfit as it struts down the runway. This will help you get started: "Spot the Cow looks fabulous in the latest Paris fashions. On her four hooves, she's wearing…"

VOCAB BOOST **chic (noun):** style

Why did the superhero wear such big shoes?

ANSWER: **Because of his amazing feats!**

feat (noun): an important accomplishment that displays courage or skill

 Tell the story of the Crime Stomper, a superhero who wears very large shoes. What remarkable deeds has he or she performed? In other words, describe the feats of someone with very big feet. Tell Crime Stomper's story in comic book form, if you'd like.

Where would you go to buy really weird stuff?

ANSWER: **A bazaar**

bazaar (noun): a street market with a variety of shops or stalls; a sale of items to raise money

Writing Prompt

Imagine a market called the Bizarre Bazaar. It's full of strange shops such as Bubbles 'R' Us, which sells nothing but bubble gum and bubble bath. Think of at least ten other shops you might find at this bazaar. Give them interesting names, and write brief descriptions of each.

VOCAB BOOST **bizarre (adjective):** very strange and unusual

---

What do you call a woodpecker with a sense of style?

ANSWER: **Impeccable**

impeccable (adjective): perfect; without flaws

Writing Prompt

Often the word *impeccable* is used to describe people's outfits. A woman wearing a stylish business suit might be described as "impeccably dressed." Describe an outfit that you think is impeccable. It can be anything: the perfect clothing for a formal party or for a summer barbecue or even for hanging out at the mall. Then draw a picture to go with your description.

VOCAB BOOST **flaw (noun):** a mistake, fault, or shortcoming, often minor

Vocabulary-Boosting Jokes & Riddles Scholastic Teaching Resources

What did Dela wear?

ANSWER: Her New Jersey

jersey (noun): a pullover shirt

 Writing Prompt People often wear jerseys when they are playing sports such as football or soccer. Write an exciting sports story in which you recount the action of a real or imagined game. Include a brief description of each team's jersey.

What do you call a lazy shoe?

ANSWER: A loafer

loafer (noun): one that is lazy or idle

 Writing Prompt By one definition, a loafer is a lazy person. Loafer is also a trademarked term for a casual shoe that you can step into. Imagine that you started a company called Loafers for Loafers. Write a silly advertising jingle to sell this style of shoe.

 VOCAB BOOST **Loafer™ (noun):** a low, casual shoe

What do you call a confused bobcat?

ANSWER: Discombobulated

discombobulated (adjective): bewildered; mixed-up; confused

Discombobulated is a long, complicated word and it has all kinds of other words hidden inside of it. For example, there's *disco* and *late*, just to name a couple. See how many words you can find hidden inside *discombobulated*. Then write a story using those words. Don't worry: It doesn't matter if your story is somewhat discombobulated.

What word describes a group of animals in complete agreement?

ANSWER: Unanimous

unanimous (adjective): agreeing; having the consent of all

Politicians try to persuade people to agree with them. They hope the agreement will be unanimous. Think of an issue you feel strongly about. It could be cleaning up litter or the need for more stop signs on city streets. Pretend you are running for political office. Write a brief speech in which you try to convince people to agree with your views.

 consent (noun): agreement; approval
consent (verb): to agree; to approve

What do you call a member of the Mallards Hall of Fame?

ANSWER: **An inductee**

inductee (noun): one who is chosen as a member

 What if you could start your own hall of fame? It could be for anything: professional wrestlers, cartoon characters, rap musicians. Who would you choose as your first five inductees? Why? What exhibits would you display at your hall of fame?

 mallard (noun): a common duck found in the wild

What do you call a very energetic ram?

ANSWER: **Rambunctious**

rambunctious (adjective): wild, disorderly; full of energy

Writing Prompt If there are rambunctious rams, there must be other animals such as sarcastic seals or annoyed aardvarks. See if you can write down an entire alphabet's worth of animals, from angry anteaters to zany zebras.

VOCAB BOOST **ram (noun):** a male sheep

What do you call a fight between two snails?

ANSWER: **A slugfest**

slugfest (noun): a fight or battle

 Imagine that you are the announcer for a wrestling match between two snails, Pokey and Slider. Write a play-by-play describing the action. This will help you get started: "In the near corner, weighing in at two ounces, with a bright red shell featuring blue stripes, is the defending world champion, Pokey the Snail...."

What do you call a farm animal that provides money instead of milk?

ANSWER: **A cash cow**

cash cow (noun): a reliable business or other source of money

 If there is such a thing as a cash cow, couldn't there also be a marmalade moose or a cheddar cheese chicken? Think of a few imaginary animals and write a silly poem about them.

What do you call a really grouchy stuffed animal?

ANSWER: Unbearable

unbearable (adjective): difficult to put up with, intolerable

Writing Prompt Finish the story "Bartholomew Bear's Unbearable Day." This will help you get started: "First, the alarm didn't ring, so Bartholomew hibernated much too long. When he finally awoke, someone had eaten all his porridge. Next,…"

VOCAB BOOST **tolerable (adjective):** good enough; agreeable

What do you call a hippopotamus that says one thing but does another?

ANSWER: A hypocrite

hypocrite (noun): a person who behaves falsely, claiming to believe one thing but then doing something different

Writing Prompt Imagine a guy named Biff who tells everyone that he loves to read novels. But in fact, he hasn't picked up a novel in ten years. Instead he reads comic books. Think of three other situations in which someone is acting like a hypocrite. Describe what the person is doing and why you think he or she is behaving that way.

What do you call a calm porcupine?

ANSWER: Tranquil

tranquil (adjective): calm; peaceful

 Haikus are a form of Japanese poetry. Often they are about nature and they usually create a very tranquil mood. Haikus are three lines long. They have five syllables in the first line, seven syllables in the second, and five syllables in the last line. The lines don't rhyme. Here's an example:

> Rainbow up above,
> soft and beautiful colors
> light the morning sky.

Now you try writing a haiku. Make it nice and tranquil!

What do you call it when a black-and-white bear goes wild?

ANSWER: Pandemonium

pandemonium (noun): extreme confusion and noise; chaos

 Pretend you are writing a brochure for the local zoo. Give names to the various exhibits, and write a sentence or two about each. Make them sound exciting so that people will be interested in visiting. Use colorful language, such as "It's panda pandemonium at the Panda Palace! You'll have a wild time!"

VOCAB BOOST **chaos (noun):** complete disorder

What kind of newspaper does a gazelle read?

ANSWER: **A gazette**

gazette (noun): a newspaper

Writing Prompt

Create the front page of a newspaper for your school. Call it the [your school's name] Gazette. Write headlines for your school's most important news. Then write a story or two as well. You might work with a small group of students and together create an entire newspaper.

VOCAB BOOST

gazelle (noun): a type of small, fast antelope found in Africa and Asia

What do you call a cow with ups and downs?

ANSWER: **Moody**

moody (adjective): subject to frequent emotional changes; depressed, unhappy

Writing Prompt

How many different moods can you think of? Make a list with words such as *gleeful*, *dismayed*, *frustrated*, and so on. Look in a thesaurus to come up with interesting words that describe a full range of moods. Then use your list to create a poem, short story, or song that includes as many of the words from your list as possible.

VOCAB BOOST

mood (noun): an emotional state such as happiness, sadness, or anger

When did Benjamin Franklin discover that lightning contains electricity?

ANSWER: During a brainstorm.

brainstorm (noun): a quick and clever idea

Writing Prompt Imagine that throughout the year, your school will be raising money for a charity. In a small group, work together to come up with a plan. Brainstorm as many ideas as you can for raising as much money as possible. Write all the ideas down, then go back and discuss each one. Which fundraising ideas do you think will be the most successful?

VOCAB BOOST **brainstorm (verb):** to share ideas or solve a problem as a group

"I do not agree that King Kong is cooler than King Tut. I strongly disagree. I wish to re_____."

ANSWER: Rebut

rebut (verb): to offer the opposite point of view in an argument or debate

Writing Prompt Consider the following statement: "It is important to get revenge. If someone wrongs you, you should always make a point of getting that person back." What do you think of this idea? Write a rebuttal in which you take the opposite point of view.

VOCAB BOOST **rebuttal (noun):** an argument that tries to show that an idea is false or wrong

Why was the ghost prevented from scaring people?

ANSWER: It was taboo.

taboo (adjective): socially unacceptable; forbidden

Writing Prompt In some cultures, it is considered taboo to slurp your soup. In other cultures, it is considered taboo not to slurp your soup. After all, loud, happy smacking noises are a sign that people are enjoying the meal. Which do you agree with? Now pretend you are writing a guide to good manners. Give your arguments either for or against soup slurping.

What do you call a confused minus sign?

ANSWER: Nonplussed

nonplussed (adjective): bewildered, puzzled, or confused

 Writing Prompt What makes you feel nonplussed? Think about words, ideas, or situations that you find strange or puzzling. For example, why do *flammable* and *inflammable* both mean the same thing? They sound like opposites, right? Create a list of at least three items and explain what is confusing about each.

What kind of attitude does a castle have?

ANSWER: **Fortitude**

. . . .

fortitude (noun): mental strength and courage

 Fortitude is not such a common word. But it describes a personal trait that is very desirable. Write a brief essay on the importance of fortitude. Provide some examples of times when fortitude is useful.

VOCAB BOOST **fortify (verb):** to make stronger; to enrich

What do you call a problem that involves itching?

ANSWER: **A glitch**

. . . .

glitch (noun): a small problem; something that goes wrong

Writing Prompt Mel and his dad have set their alarms for 6 A.M. They want to get up early to search for earthworms for Mel's science project. They plan to use flashlights to find worms in the backyard. But they encounter a glitch. Can you imagine what problems Mel and his dad might encounter? Write about the glitch (or glitches) in their plans.

How did the students feel about the eight-hour exam?

ANSWER: **They detested it.**

detest (verb): to dislike strongly

Writing Prompt

Have you ever noticed that it is more fun to describe a negative opinion than a positive one? After all, how many ways can you really say that you like something? But explaining why you strongly dislike something can be highly pleasurable: You get to use words like *abhor* and *repulsive* and *detest*. What type of food do you detest? Write a review of that food, and spice it up with lots of colorful negative words.

VOCAB BOOST
abhor (verb): to dislike strongly; to loathe
repulsive (adjective): disgusting

What do you call a brother and sister who hiss?

ANSWER: **Sibilant siblings**

sibilant (adjective): producing a hissing sound

Writing Prompt
Write a Sibilant Story. It could feature a sneaky snake or Super Sam or a silly sailor. Simply use lots of s's, so that when you read the story aloud, you'll sound like you're hissing.

VOCAB BOOST
sibling (noun): a brother or sister

What do you call an extremely angry 18-wheeler?

ANSWER: Truculent

truculent (adjective): cruel, mean-spirited

Writing Prompt

Truculent is what people jokingly call a five-dollar word. There are plenty of simpler synonyms such as *spiteful*, *nasty*, and *mean*. But sometimes it's fun to roll out a big fancy word like *truculent*. Imagine two friends named Giles and Bartholomew. Whenever they argue, they toss around all kinds of five-dollar words. Write some dialogue for this pair. The following exchange will help you get started:

Giles: You appear to be in a truculent mood today, Bart.

Bart: Oh, Giles, cease with your disparaging remarks.

VOCAB BOOST

cease (verb): to stop immediately

disparaging (adjective): unkindly critical

How did you trick the whole class into believing your incredible story?

ANSWER: It took quite a wile!

wile (noun): a clever and deceptive trick

Writing Prompt

A person who exercises wile is said to be wily. In fact, there's a famous cartoon character named Wily Coyote. Come up with a new character, such as Wily Anteater or Wily Donkey. Write a brief story about your character. If you like, write it in comic book form.

VOCAB BOOST

deceptive (adjective): misleading

wily (adjective): full of tricks

What does a wheel wear to a fancy event?

ANSWER: **Formal attire**

attire (noun): clothing

 Someone who purchases outfits for circus performers might be called a high-wire attire buyer. Dream up at least five other rhyming job titles. Then write a description of each.

 formal (adjective): proper; following established rules or customs; official

What do you call a nail that always knows the right thing to say?

ANSWER: **Tactful**

tactful (adjective): having or showing skill and sensitivity in dealing with people

 Being tactful comes in handy in all kinds of situations. Say someone was talking during a movie. A person sitting nearby could be tactful and say, "I would appreciate it if you would kindly stop talking." Or the person could show less tact and say, "Do you mind? I'm missing half the movie!" Think of three other situations in which a person could show tact. Describe the situation and write a tactful response to each.

 tact (noun): skill in dealing with others; the ability to speak and act appropriately

What do you call an arrogant sponge?

ANSWER: **Self-absorbed**

. . . .

self-absorbed (adjective): excessively interested or involved in one's own self

 In addition to self-absorbed, the English language has lots of "self" words. *Self-assured* means confident. *Self-pity* means feeling sorry for yourself. Look up the "self" words in the dictionary, and choose several that you like or find useful. Use at least five of them in a poem, brief story, or essay. Include the word *self-absorbed* as one of the five.

 arrogant (adjective): having an overdeveloped sense of one's importance

What do you call a bunch of mixed-up marbles?

ANSWER: **Garbled marbles**

. . . .

garbled (adjective): altered or changed around in a confusing way

 "Hickory mouse up the ran dock the clock dickory." The words of this familiar nursery rhyme have been garbled. Can you fix them? Garble some other famous or familiar lines or phrases. Then exchange these with your classmates to put them in the correct order.

 garble (verb): to change, distort, or mix up something

altered (adjective): changed

What does a critical lamp like to do?

ANSWER: Lampoon

lampoon (verb): to ridicule or criticize

 Writing Prompt Pretend you are hosting a party for your favorite superhero or cartoon character. You are called upon to do some lampooning. Say the Incredible Hulk was the guest of honor. You might start off with something like "Hey Hulk, you're sure looking green. Did you eat something that disagreed with you?" Remember, lampooning can be lighthearted. Poke fun, but don't get downright mean.

VOCAB BOOST **lampoon (noun):** criticism or ridicule

You're so dull.

What do you call a sleepy pile of wood?

ANSWER: Slumber

slumber (noun): sleep

Writing Prompt In Washington Irving's classic tale, Rip Van Winkle sits down at the base of a tree and falls into a deep slumber that lasts 20 years. When he wakes up, he finds that the whole world is different. Imagine that you fell into a 20-year slumber. What would have changed while you were sleeping? Write a diary entry describing what you discovered when you woke up.

VOCAB BOOST **lumber (noun):** large pieces of wood (usually sawed), such as boards or logs
slumber (verb): to sleep

What do you call a decorated bell?

ANSWER: **Embellished**

. . . .

embellish (verb): to add detail; decorate

Writing Prompt Have you ever heard the phrase "embellish a story"? It means to add a little touch or detail to make the story better. In fact, it doesn't have to be the truth. For example, historians are now pretty certain that George Washington did not actually chop down a cherry tree. But that embellishment sure makes for a good story. Think of a story that you know, real or fictional, and make some changes to improve it. In other words, embellish the story.

VOCAB BOOST **embellishment (noun):** the act of decorating or adding detail

What do you call rowdy rocks?

ANSWER: **Raucous**

. . . .

raucous (adjective): wild and loud; harsh sounding

Writing Prompt Your favorite sports team has just won the championship. The fans are going wild! All the players are jumping around screaming. It's truly a raucous scene. Pretend you're a sports reporter. It's your job to get an interview with the team's star player. What questions might you ask, and what answers might the star player provide?

VOCAB BOOST **rowdy (adjective):** noisy and out of control

What did the window say to the cute door?

ANSWER: "You're adorable!"

· ·

adorable (adjective): charming; lovable

Writing Prompt Lots of things are adorable: puppies, sunflowers, and smiles, just to name a few. The opposite of *adorable* is *despicable*. It means extremely *not* charming and *not* loveable. Make two lists with the headings "Adorable" and "Despicable." See how many items you can put in each list.

VOCAB BOOST **despicable (adjective):** worthy of being strongly disliked

adore (verb): to be very fond of

What do you call a large painting that shows a country scene?

ANSWER: A rural mural

· ·

rural (adjective): of or related to the countryside

Writing Prompt Cities are known as urban areas. Farms are found in rural areas. Rural areas have fresh air and pretty scenery. Urban areas have lots of people and buildings. Make a list comparing urban and rural areas. Write down some of the things you like about each.

VOCAB BOOST **mural (noun):** a painting painted directly on a wall or ceiling

urban (adjective): of or related to the city

What do you call a beagle that's always losing?

ANSWER: **An underdog**

underdog (noun): one that is not favored;
in sports or a contest, one that is expected to lose

Writing Prompt It's always surprising and exciting when an underdog wins. Imagine a dog show with purebred poodles and clever collies. But there's also a dog named Rex. Rex isn't well groomed and he isn't well trained. But he is so fun and friendly that he wins the blue ribbon. Write the story of Rex the Underdog.

What do you get if you cross Lassie with a watermelon?

ANSWER: **Melancholy**

melancholy (noun): a state of depression

 Writing Prompt Imagine there was a sad dog named Melon Collie and a joyful frog named Hop E. Ness. Make up a folktale about this odd pair, and tell their story.

 VOCAB BOOST **melancholy (adjective):** characterized by sadness or low spirits

Vocabulary-Boosting Jokes & Riddles Scholastic Teaching Resources

What do you call a whole bunch of little dogs?

ANSWER: **A caboodle of poodles**

caboodle (noun): a bunch or a lot

 You might encounter a caboodle of just about anything: cabooses, noodles, or apple strudels. Imagine a whole group of something— anything at all, really. What might happen to this group? What could they do or how might others react to them? Now write a creative story about this caboodle.

What kind of food does an irritable dog eat?

ANSWER: **Quibbles and bits**

quibble (noun): a small complaint or criticism

 Imagine a Web site you could visit to post small complaints about absolutely anything. What bothers you in a minor way? Remember, this site is for quibbles, not big gripes. When you create your posting, remember to keep your complaints suitably small.

 quibble (verb): to bicker or argue about unimportant matters

Dry food again!

What did the little dog say when the big dog wouldn't stop bothering him?

ANSWER: "Stop hounding me!"

hound (verb): to bother or harass

Writing Prompt

If someone is bothering you, you might say that he or she is hounding you. Wouldn't it be fun to make up other animal verbs? For example, sleeping late could be called bearing. Write down at least five animal verbs along with their definitions. Then use each in a sentence.

VOCAB BOOST

hound (noun): a dog bred for hunting

How does a stray dog speak?

ANSWER: It mutters.

mutter (verb): to speak in a low, grumbling voice, usually with the mouth almost closed

Writing Prompt

In movies, some of the best evil characters mutter. They don't have to speak loudly or clearly to get their point across. Just by looking at them, it's obvious that they're tough and mean. Dream up a movie villain and create some suitably menacing, mumbling dialogue. Hey, what are you looking at, kid? Put your pencil to paper.

Why did the man drink a glass of water before dinner?

ANSWER: It helped whet his appetite.

whet (verb): to sharpen or make stronger

 Writing Prompt Because *whet* is often used with the word *appetite*, people make a common mistake by spelling the word *wet*. The word is actually *whet*. It means to strengthen. Write a detailed description of a dish so delicious-sounding it will whet anyone's appetite. If your description is really good, it will make readers' mouths water. Then you will have succeeded in both whetting and wetting their appetites.

 VOCAB BOOST **appetite (noun):** the desire for something, usually food

What did the indecisive customer do when ordering breakfast?

ANSWER: He waffled.

waffle (verb): to continue to change one's mind or opinion; to avoid answering a question directly

 Writing Prompt Do you ever have a day when you just can't make up your mind? The kind of day when every decision causes you to waffle? Should you wear your green velour pullover or the itchy wool sweater your great-aunt knitted for you? Should you have blueberry pancakes with raspberry syrup or raspberry waffles with blueberry syrup? Imagine that you had such a day and write a short story about it.

I'll have scrambled eggs, please. Actually, make that pancakes. No, wait...

 VOCAB BOOST **waffle (noun):** a crispy cake baked in an appliance that gives it a pattern

What kind of candy do you avoid at all costs?

ANSWER: **A detriment**

detriment (noun): something that causes harm or damage

 Writing Prompt

Detriment is a noun; *detrimental* is an adjective. You certainly want to avoid detriments and things that are detrimental. Think of at least three warning labels in which you use either word. Here's an example: "This baseball is detrimental to windows and other glass items."

VOCAB BOOST **detrimental (adjective):** harmful

What do you call a big bag full of hamburger buns?

ANSWER: **Abundant**

abundant (adjective): plentiful

 Writing Prompt

Write a story about an abundance of something you like. The story can be about a meal where huge portions of all your favorite foods are served. Or it could be about discovering a secret room piled high with all your favorite games. What would you do with this abundance of goodies?

VOCAB BOOST **abundance (noun):** a large amount

What kind of sandwich doesn't get enough praise?

ANSWER: **An unsung hero**

unsung (adjective): not suitably praised or honored; not sung

 Writing Prompt

An unsung hero isn't a sandwich. It's a person who does impressive deeds but doesn't receive proper praise. Who do you think is an unsung hero? What about a bus driver, for example? Bus drivers make sure kids get to school safely, but no one ever gives them a medal. Maybe a parent or another relative counts as an unsung hero. Create an Unsung Hero Certificate for someone you think is deserving. It could begin "In honor of your dedicated service in the…"

VOCAB BOOST

hero (noun): someone who is brave or courageous; the main character in a story

hero (noun): a type of long sandwich, also called a submarine

---

What do you call an onion that likes to get into mischief?

ANSWER: **A rapscallion**

rapscallion (noun): a rascal or troublemaker

Writing Prompt

The word *rapscallion* just plain sounds like something you might call a pirate. It's one of those old-fangled words, such as *vagabond* or *knave,* that you might hear on a pirate ship. Write your own salty sea story, featuring dialogue between some mischievous characters. Here's a line for inspiration: "Unhand that gold, you seafaring rapscallion!"

VOCAB BOOST

rascal (noun): someone who causes trouble and is often mean or dishonest

scallion (noun): a type of green onion

What kind of spice gives really wise advice?

ANSWER: Sage

sage (noun): an herb used to flavor food; a wise person

 Who do you know that could be described as a sage? Maybe a grandparent or a teacher or a friend? Write about this person. Recount some of the person's wisdom in his or her actions, lessons, and sayings.

 sage (adjective): marked by wisdom and good judgment

What kind of house does a hot dog live in?

ANSWER: A bungalow

bungalow (noun): a small house, usually one-story high

Writing Prompt What kind of home would you like to live in? Maybe you'd like to live in a huge castle with one entire room used only to store fruit roll-ups, or perhaps you'd prefer a country cottage where you could see wild deer grazing in the backyard. There are plenty of choices. Write a description of your dream home.

Vocabulary-Boosting Jokes & Riddles Scholastic Teaching Resources

What do you call crumbs that are very delicious?

ANSWER: **Scrumptious**

scrumptious (adjective): truly tasty; delightful

Writing Prompt Doesn't the word *scrumptious* seem made up? It sounds like someone simply took a bite of hot apple pie and blurted, "Mmmm, this is scrumptious!" So why not make up words like *bellyicious* (food so good you want some in your belly) and *wunning* (walking so fast you're nearly running). Write a story using at least ten made-up words. Be sure to include a key with the definitions so that other people can understand your story.

What do you call a fake ham?

ANSWER: **A sham**

sham (noun): something that is false or fake

Writing Prompt Pretend that you have a Web site that helps expose shams: toys that don't do what they're supposed to, clothing that rips easily, appliances that don't work. For the Web site, write about something that you consider to be a sham. This useful service will protect other people from similar scams and shams.

VOCAB BOOST **sham (adjective):** false
sham (verb): to fake something; to give the wrong impression

What kind of excuse would you find at the beginning of a book?

ANSWER: **A pretext**

• •

pretext (noun): a given reason or an excuse

Writing Prompt You are supposed to be doing your chores. But you want to visit your friend instead. Invent a pretext. Make it as wild and elaborate as you possibly can.

VOCAB BOOST **text (noun):** the main writing in a book or on a page

pre-: The prefix *pre-* means "before." For example, *precede* means "to come before."

How is the letter *u* different from the rest?

ANSWER: **It's unique.**

• •

unique (adjective): the only one of its kind; different than the others

Writing Prompt If you look at snowflakes under a magnifying glass, you'll see that every one is different. Each snowflake is unique. What about people? There are billions of people in the world. Do you think every single one is in some way unique? Answer this question in a brief essay.

What do you call someone who uses too many verbs and other words?

ANSWER: Verbose

verbose (adjective): using an excessive number of words

Writing Prompt Have you ever noticed how simple most signs are? A stop sign uses a single word so that people get the message quickly. But what if a verbose person redesigned the stop sign? It might read: "At this point, you must bring your car or motorcycle or bicycle to a complete halt." You get the idea. Be verbose. Take a simple sign or command and rework it into something that is ridiculously long-winded. I wish you a great amount of what is generally but not always referred to as luck.

What kind of stationery never moves?

ANSWER: The stationary kind

stationary (adjective): not moving; not changing

Writing Prompt One good thing about stationary objects is that they are easy to look at. You can really study them carefully. Look at something stationary like a pencil or a building and describe it in as much detail as you can.

VOCAB BOOST **stationery (noun):** paper and envelopes for writing letters

What kind of special language do bingo players use?

ANSWER: Lingo

lingo (noun): unfamiliar language, such as the specialized vocabulary used for a certain job or activity

Writing Prompt Baseball has its own lingo: *strikeout, foul ball, home run.* Movies have a lingo: *special effects, cut, chase scene.* When you write, using appropriate lingo can help make a story more convincing. What activity do you know a lot about? Write about it, being sure to use lots of lingo.

Wigglesworth Razzmattaz Grigsby de Grume—that happened to be the writer's nom de _____.

ANSWER: plume

nom de plume (noun): pen name (a name that an author uses instead of his or her real name)

Writing Prompt Theodor Seuss Geisel's *nom de plume* was Dr. Seuss. Samuel Clemens's was Mark Twain. Give yourself a *nom de plume.* You can make it simple or you can make it long and fancy. Then write a short story under your new pen name.

 VOCAB BOOST **pseudonym (noun):** a false name; a pen name

If a fallen tree delivered a speech, what would it be called?

ANSWER: **A monologue**

monologue (noun): a long speech given by one person
(in the case of a comedian, a series of jokes)

Writing Prompt You are writing a play called The Solid Gold Toothpick. This is the dramatic moment. The rare and precious golden toothpick has just been discovered in the pocket of a character named Count TuTenn. Write a monologue for Count TuTenn. Make it long and colorful, and have the count provide all kinds of excuses and explanations for why the golden toothpick was found in his possession.

How do you leave a secret message in a tomb?

ANSWER: **You encrypt it.**

encrypt (verb): to put something into code

Writing Prompt Create your own encryption. For example, the letter *A* could be replaced by the number 1, the letter *B* by the number 2, and so forth. Write an encrypted message. Then exchange messages with classmates to see if they can crack your code. Remember to create a key so that you'll remember how to decode your message.

VOCAB BOOST **encryption (noun):** something written in code

crypt (noun): an underground room, often for burial

What do you call a monster with really good hearing?

ANSWER: **Eerie**

eerie (adjective): mysterious in an unsettling or frightening way

Writing Prompt Have you ever read a story or a part of a book that made you feel uneasy? How did the author do this? Create your own eerie scene. Try to build the reader's suspense. This will help you get started: "The house on the hill was dark and abandoned. The front door creaked as it opened, and inside..."

At what temperature does Luke Skywalker prefer his tea?

ANSWER: **Lukewarm**

lukewarm (adjective): slightly warm; lacking enthusiasm

Writing Prompt *Lukewarm* is a strange word, right? Maybe there should be other combinations of names and temperatures. For example, what if *crystalcold* meant ice cold? Come up with at least three different name-temperature combinations. Then pretend you're a weather person on television. Write a weather report using the new words you've made up.

What do you call a spare space alien?

ANSWER: **An extraterrestrial**

extraterrestrial (noun): a creature that is not from the planet Earth

 Writing Prompt Imagine that an extraterrestrial visited your hometown. What would it look like? Would it be friendly? What would it do? Write a newspaper article describing a visit by an extraterrestrial. Remember to answer the questions: Who? What? Where? When? How? and Why?

VOCAB BOOST **extraterrestrial (adjective):** originating from outer space

What's an eye doctor's favorite part of the writing process?

ANSWER: **Revision**

revision (noun): the act of changing or reworking something; a changed or updated version

 Writing Prompt Can you think of a book, movie, or TV show that's okay, but could be improved? What changes would you make? What would you do differently? Write down some revisions that you would like to see.

 VOCAB BOOST **revise (verb):** to change, correct, or update something

What do you call a dull person walking down the street?

ANSWER: **A pedestrian**

....

pedestrian (adjective): dull; uninteresting

Writing Prompt

As a noun, *pedestrian* refers to a person who walks. But the adjective is used to describe something that is dull. A paper clip might be described as a pedestrian object. Now here's your challenge: Write an exciting story involving a paper clip or another pedestrian object.

VOCAB BOOST

pedestrian (noun): a person who is walking

pedestrian (adjective): having to do with walking (a pedestrian walkway)

What did the umpire shout when the chicken swung the bat?

ANSWER: "Fowl ball!"

....

fowl (noun): a bird, usually one raised for food, such as a chicken or turkey

Writing Prompt

Something that is difficult to define can be described as "neither fish nor fowl." Say for example, you saw someone riding a bicycle with wings. It wouldn't exactly be a plain old bicycle. But it wouldn't be an airplane either. Describe an invention of your own that falls somewhere in the middle—that's neither fish nor fowl.

VOCAB BOOST

foul (adjective): against the rules or out of bounds; offensive, unpleasant, dirty, or disgusting

What did the boy do when he outgrew his bed?

ANSWER: **He boycotted it.**

boycott (verb): to refuse to do something (such as buying a product) as a protest

Writing Prompt If you don't like something about a particular store or business, you can decide to boycott it. This means that you choose not to buy their products or services. People often do this as a way of protesting. Their goal is for the store or business to change its ways. What would cause you to boycott a store or business? Describe what you would do and why.

Why do some trees lose their leaves every autumn?

ANSWER: **It's their routine.**

routine (noun): a sequence of actions one regularly follows

Writing Prompt Are there a series of things you do each morning to get ready for school? Or maybe there is a set of steps you always follow to clean out your aquarium. This is called a routine. Write a detailed description of one of your routines.

 VOCAB BOOST **routine (adjective):** normal, ordinary, not unusual

What do you call a silent mother?

ANSWER: Mum

mum (adjective): not talking; silent

 The word *mum* is an example of a palindrome. Palindromes are words that are the same whether they are spelled forward or backward. Other palindromes include *radar*, *Bob*, *tot*, and *noon*. Think of as many palindromes as you can. Then use them in a Palindrome Poem.

VOCAB BOOST **mum (noun):** a chrysanthemum (a type of flower)

Why did the boy enjoy looking at the construction site?

ANSWER: It was riveting.

riveting (adjective): extremely interesting; fascinating

 Construction workers join pieces of metal with bolts called rivets. The word *riveting* is used to describe something so fascinating, you can't help but pay attention. If you're watching a riveting movie, it's as if your eyes are attached to the screen. Can you see how the word *riveting* is related to the word *rivet*? Write a Riveting Rap. Make it so interesting and exciting that people have no choice but to stop and listen.

VOCAB BOOST **rivet (noun):** a type of metal bolt used in construction work to join things

Vocabulary-Boosting Jokes & Riddles Scholastic Teaching Resources

Where do you go to mail letters to people living in the year 2200?

ANSWER: **The posterity office**

posterity (noun): future generations of people

Writing Prompt When the founders of the United States drew up the U.S. Constitution, they were thinking of posterity. They created a document that would apply to people many generations into the future. Now write your own document, a Personal Constitution. Include rules and values that you think are important. As you draft your Personal Constitution, consider how it might be important to posterity.

Why does 11 o'clock come after 10 o'clock?

ANSWER: **It's chronological.**

chronological (adjective): organized by time

Writing Prompt Put the events of your day in chronological order. Here's an example: "7:30 A.M., woke up. 7:45 A.M., ate breakfast...." Think hard and try to remember the various events of your day and what time they occurred. Be as detailed as possible.

What do you call a bugle player who doesn't waste a cent?

ANSWER: **A frugal player**

frugal (adjective): wise and sparing about using things; not wasteful; thrifty

Writing Prompt Imagine you had $100 to spend. Write out a budget, listing all the things you would buy and how much each costs. Remember to be frugal. Really try to stretch your money and make it go a long way.

VOCAB BOOST **thrifty (adjective):** economical; careful not to waste resources

What do you call a mushroom that's in a good mood?

ANSWER: **A fungus**

fungus (noun): a member of the family of plants that includes molds and mushrooms

Writing Prompt "It's the yellow fungus bus!" What in the world does that mean? Well, you decide. Write a story that features someone saying that line. Have fun, or rather, have fungus!

Vocabulary-Boosting Jokes & Riddles Scholastic Teaching Resources